Draw Your Own Encyclopaedia

Our Solar System

Colin M. Drysdale

Illustrated by ______________________________

Pictish Beast Publications

ISBN - 978-1-909832-46-6
Published by Pictish Beast Publications, Glasgow, UK.
Published in the United Kingdom
First Printing: 2018. First Edition.

www.PictishBeastPublications.com

How To Use This Book

This is a *Draw Your Own Encyclopaedia* book for children aged six to twelve. It will provide you with interesting introductions to a variety of different features of our solar system, along with quick facts, questions you can answer and, at the end, a pop quiz where you can test the knowledge of our solar system which you have gained by reading this book. So far, this may seem like any other book of facts, but unlike almost every other such book, you are allowed to draw in this one. In fact, you are actively encouraged to do so! Through this, you will become the illustrator of your very own encyclopaedia chapter all about our solar system.

When adding your own pictures to this book, it is important that you seek out suitable images to base your own ones on. This can be done either by consulting other books, or by entering an appropriate search term into an internet search engine (such as *Google*). If you choose to use an internet search engine, the best results will usually be achieved by entering a simple search term followed by the word picture. For example, for the illustration on page two, the best search term to use would be *Solar system Picture.*

For Parents And Educators

To help ensure your child's safety online, please use appropriate online safety procedures and supervise their internet usage at all times when looking for pictures on which they can base their illustrations for this book. You can also use this time to discuss internet safety with your child, as well as strategies for searching for specific information, and how to decide whether information they find on the internet is reliable or not.

If you wish to use any of the contents of this book for educational purposes, an educational licence (which allows you to legally photocopy pages to create handouts) can be purchased from *www.pictishbeastpublications.com/ draw-your-own-encyclopaedi*a. Ideas for classroom activities to accompany this book can also be accessed through this webpage.

What Is A Solar System?

A solar system consists of a star and all the objects in space that orbit around it. Our solar system formed around 4.6 billion years ago from a cloud of interstellar dust left over from the explosion of an older, and much larger, star. Today, our solar system consists of our sun, 8 planets, 525 moons, and many hundreds of thousands of minor planets, asteroids and comets. It is approximately 287.46 billion kilometres in diameter. However, because it travels so fast, it only takes light from the sun about six days to reach the edge of the solar system!

Quick Fact: The sun is actually a star. While it has no official scientific name, it is sometimes referred to by the Latin name Sol.

Quick Fact: The nearest neighbouring solar system is called Proxima Centauri. It is approximately 40 trillion kilometres away!

How old is our solar system?

Draw a picture of our solar system showing the sun at the centre and the relative positions of the eight planets that orbit around it. Write down the name of each planet beside it.

What Is The Largest Planet In Our Solar System?

The largest planet in our solar system is Jupiter. It is 139,822 kilometres in diameter and weighs the same as 318 planet Earths. This means that while it is a thousand times lighter than the sun, its mass is two and a half times the mass of all the other planets in the solar system combined. Jupiter is what is known as a gas giant. This means it does not have a solid surface and is mainly made from a mixture of gases and liquids. Jupiter is 139,822 km away from the sun, and it takes almost twelve Earth years to complete a single orbit of the sun.

<u>Quick Fact</u>: The smallest planet in our solar system is Mercury. It is 4,879 kilometres in diameter. This means that it is one-third the size of the Earth.

What is the largest planet in our solar system? What is the smallest? Draw pictures of these two planets side by side, using the same scale for each one so you can see how different they are in size.

Quick Fact: Jupiter is famous for its Great Red Spot. This is a storm that has been raging in its atmosphere for at least 188 years, and possibly much, much longer. It is 16,350 kilometres in diameter, making this single storm larger than the whole of planet Earth!

Is Pluto A Planet?

Until very recently, Pluto was considered to be the ninth planet in our solar system. However, in 2006, the International Astronomical Union downgraded its classification to a dwarf planet. For an object to be considered a full planet, it must fulfil three criteria: 1. It must orbit the sun; 2. It must have a sufficient mass that gravity makes it form a more-or-less round shape; 3. It has to have cleared its orbit of other objects. While Pluto orbits the sun and is more-or-less round, there are other objects which share its orbit, meaning it isn't big enough to have cleared these objects away.

__Quick Fact__: Pluto is one of five dwarf planets that have so far been given names. The others are Ceres, Haumea, Makemake and Eris. However, there may be several hundred more out there that have yet to be given official names.

What are the three things a space object has to do to be considered a planet?

1.
2.
3.

Draw pictures of Pluto here, and under it, write its name. See if you can find out how big it is, and write its diameter down alongside its name.

<u>**Quick Fact**</u>: Pluto was only discovered in 1930 by Clyde Tombaugh of the Lowell Observatory in Flagstaff, Arizona, USA. It was named after the ancient Greek god of the underworld. The name was first suggested by Venetia Burney who, at the time, was eleven years old.

How Hot Is The Sun?

The sun is almost 200,000 kilometres in diameter, and it is effectively a very large ball of burning gas. It is primarily made of hydrogen, and its heat and light are generated by the fusion of hydrogen nuclei to form helium. The surface of the sun is around 5,500 degrees centigrade. That makes it 10 times hotter than the coals in a barbecue. The light from the sun travels at 299,792 kilometres per second, and despite the 146 million kilometres that separate the Sun from the Earth, it only takes eight minutes for its light to reach us.

<u>Quick Fact</u>: The surface is not the hottest part of the sun. In solar flares, which are eruptions of hot gas, temperatures can reach up to 100 million degrees!

<u>Quick Fact</u>: One of the coldest places in the solar system is the south-western edge of Hermite Crater on the Moon. Here, temperatures can be as low as -247 °C.

As well as generating heat and light, the sun also generates a solar wind. These are charged particles that stream out from it. When they hit the Earth's magnetic fields, they create the northern and southern lights. Draw a picture here to show what the northern lights look like.

<u>Quick Fact</u>: It takes the light from the sun only three minutes to reach Mercury (the closest planet) and just over four hours to reach Neptune (the furthest planet). However, it takes the sun's light four years to reach Alpha Centauri, our closest neighbouring star!

Which Planet Has The Longest Day?

A day is defined as the length of time it takes a planet to complete one full spin on its axis. On Earth, this takes just under twenty-four hours. However, on different planets, days have different lengths. At just under ten hours, Jupiter has the shortest days, while on Venus (which has the longest days) each day lasts 5,832 hours (or 243 Earth days!). A year (the time it takes a planet to complete a single orbit around the sun) also varies between planets. Mercury takes only 88 Earth days to orbit the sun, while the Earth takes 365 days. In contrast, it takes 164.8 Earth years for Neptune to complete one orbit!

Venus takes 243 Earth days to rotate once on its axis, but it only takes just under 225 Earth days to orbit the Sun. This means that on Venus, a day is longer than a year! Draw a picture of Venus here, and write its day length and year length underneath it.

Quick Fact: Venus is unusual in another way too. While almost all planets in our solar system rotate clockwise, it rotates in the opposite direction. This means that unlike on Earth, on Venus, the Sun rises in the west and sets in the east!

What Is An Asteroid?

Asteroids are pieces of rock that orbit the Sun, but which are too small to be considered planets. Asteroids must have a diameter of at least one metre, and can be as large as tens or hundreds of kilometres across. They are only found in the inner solar system, and most of them are found in the Asteroid Belt between Mars and Jupiter. Rocky asteroid-like objects are also found in the outer solar system, especially in the Kuiper Belt (which is beyond the orbit of Neptune) and in the Oort Cloud at the very edge of our solar system. However, despite their similarities, these are no longer classified as asteroids.

__Quick Fact__: The many craters that can be seen on the surface of the moon were created by asteroids hitting it.

__Quick Fact__: An asteroid hitting the Earth is thought to have been one of the main factors that caused the extinction of the dinosaurs!

Where are most asteroids in our solar system found?.

The asteroid that caused the extinction of the dinosaurs is thought to have been between ten and fifteen kilometres in diameter. Draw a picture of what you think this impact would have looked like when it happened.

Where Do Comets Come From?

Unlike asteroids, which are made of rock, comets are mostly made of ice. Most comets in our solar system come from the Oort Cloud, a vast ring containing millions of objects at the very edge of our solar system. Many of these objects are thought to have been formed at the very birth of our solar system. Occasionally, the orbit of one of these objects is disturbed, sending it shooting towards the sun. As it enters the inner solar system, the heat from the sun starts to melt it, creating a long tail of debris and making it much more easily visible.

__Quick Fact__: One of the most famous comets in the solar system is Halley's comet. It was discovered in 1705 by Edmund Halley. It is a short-period comet, meaning that it takes less than 200 Earth years to orbit the sun. Halley's comet was last seen from Earth in 1986, and it is expected to return again in the 2060s.

Halley's comet visits the inner solar system approximately once every seventy-six years. In the past, it was often seen as a predictor that something either very good or very bad was about to happen. Draw a picture of Halley's comet, with its long tail, as it appeared last time it visited the inner solar system in 1986.

<u>Quick Fact</u>: Much of the water on Earth is thought to have come from icy comets that collided with it when it was still very young.

<u>Quick Fact</u>: No matter the direction it is moving in, a comet's tail always points away from the Sun.

How Long Would It Take To Get To Mars?

Earth and Mars are neighbouring planets in the solar system, but working out how long it would take to get from Earth to Mars is not as easy as it may seem. This is because both the Earth and Mars orbit the Sun. When the Earth and Mars are both on the same side of the Sun, they are under 60 million kilometres apart. When they are on opposite sides, they are up to 250 million kilometres away from each other. In theory, our fastest space craft could get to Mars in as little as 40 days, but its launch would need to be timed perfectly. In practice, however, it would probably take between 150 and 250 days.

While no humans have visited Mars so far, we have sent a wide range of unmanned space craft there. This includes the ones that carried the Mars Rovers. These are semi-autonomous vehicles that we used to help us learn more about Mars. Draw a picture here of one of these Rovers surveying the surface of Mars.

Quick Fact: Mars is known as the red planet because it is covered in a layer of red dust. This red dust is mostly made of iron, and it's red because it has become oxidised by exposure to the thin Martian atmosphere. Here on Earth, we call this type of red dust rust, so Mars is not only the red planet, it is also the rusty planet!.

Is There Life On Other Planets In Our Solar System?

Since Earth is teeming with life, it's only reasonable to wonder if there's also life elsewhere in our solar system. Scientists have spent many years looking for life on other planets, but so far, they have yet to find any definitive evidence of life anywhere other than on Earth. However, this does not mean that there isn't life elsewhere. It might just mean it hasn't been found yet. Of all the places in the solar system where there could be life, the most likely places are on Mars, on some of the moons of Jupiter and Saturn, or even on Pluto. These places all either have, or had, liquid environments which could host microbial life.

If life does exist elsewhere in our solar system, what do you think it would look like? Would it look the same as life on Earth, or would it look very different because of very different conditions on other planets? Draw a picture of what you think alien life might look like here.

<u>**Quick Fact**</u>: For the first billion years of life on Earth, the only living things were microorganisms.

<u>**Quick Fact**</u>: If Earth is the only place in the solar system where there life exists, then it makes it all the more important to protect it!

Do Other Planets Have Moons?

A moon is an object which directly orbits another object in space other than the Sun. Most people are familiar with the Earth's moon (also known as Luna, its Latin name), but it is only one of 525 known moons in the solar system. The only planets that don't have any moons are the two that are closest to the Sun (Mercury and Venus), while Mars has two moons. In contrast, Saturn has at least sixty-two moons, and Jupiter has at least sixty-nine, including Europa and Callisto, which are both potential candidates for places where life could exist beyond Earth.

Quick Fact: Of the 525 known moons in the solar system, only 178 orbit planets. The rest orbit minor planetary bodies, including the dwarf planets of Pluto (which has five moons), Haumes (2), Makemake (1) and Eris (1).

While our Moon seems very big to us, it is not the largest moon in the Solar System. Instead, the largest moon is called Ganymede and it orbits Jupiter. Ganymede has a diameter of over 5,000 kilometres, making it twice as big as our moon, and larger than the planet Mercury! Draw a picture of Ganymede here.

__Quick Fact__: The moon is the only place in the Solar System other than Earth that humans have visited. Between 1969 and 1972, the moon was visited on six occasions, and only twelve people have ever set foot on it. The longest time anyone has ever stayed on the moon was just over three days.

What Will Happen When The Sun Runs Out Of Fuel?

The main fuel that keeps the sun burning is hydrogen, and it burns around 600 million tons of it per second. However, there is enough hydrogen left in the Sun to keep it going for another five billion years. Once all its fuel has been used up, the Sun will turn into a type of star known as a red giant. As it does this, its outer layer will expand and engulf Mercury, Venus and even the Earth. This outer layer will eventually drift off into space, leaving just the exposed core, which will form a star type known as a white dwarf and then a black dwarf, which is essentially the remnant of a dead star.

What type of star will the sun turn into in around five billion years?

Currently, the Sun is classified as a yellow dwarf star. As it uses up its fuel, it will turn into a red giant, then a white dwarf and finally a black dwarf. Draw this evolutionary sequence of the sun, making sure that you draw each star type to the same scale.

Quick Fact: By the time that the Sun turns into a red giant, and consumes the Earth, humans may well have developed the technology to be able to move to another planet, and possibly even one in another solar system. This means that even when the Sun dies, humanity may well be able to carry on.

Pop Quiz

The answers to all these questions can be found elsewhere in this book. See if you can answer them all!

1. What type of star is the Sun?
2. Which planet has the most moons?
3. How many planets are there in our solar system?
4. How big is our solar system?
5. What is the largest planet in our solar system?
6. What will happen when the Sun runs out of fuel?
7. How hot is the surface of the Sun?
8. Where is one of the coldest places in our solar system?
9. Where do most comets in our solar system come from?
10. What is an asteroid?
11. How fast does light from the Sun travel?
12. Can you name four places in our solar system other than Earth where some form of life might exist?
13. Which planet has the shortest day?
14. Why is Pluto no longer considered to be a planet?
15. What is the smallest planet in our solar system?
16. Which planet has the longest year?

Write Your Answers Here:

1. ____
2. ____
3. ____
4. ____
5. ____
6. ____
7. ____
8. ____
9. ____
10. ____
11. ____
12. ____
13. ____
14. ____
15. ____
16. ____

Pop Quiz – The Answers

1. Our sun is classified as a yellow dwarf star.
2. The planet with the most moons is Jupiter. At the last count, it had sixty-nine known moons.
3. There are eight planets in our solar system. These are Mercury, Venus, Earth, Mars, Jupiter, Saturn, Uranus and Neptune.
4. Our solar system is approximately 287.46 billion kilometres in diameter.
5. The largest planet in our solar system is Jupiter. It is 139,822 kilometres in diameter and weighs the same as 318 planet Earths.
6. When the Sun runs out of fuel, it will turn first into a red giant, then a white dwarf and, finally, a black dwarf.
7. The surface of the sun is 5,500 degrees centigrade.
8. One of the coldest place in our solar system is the south-western edge of Hermite Crater on the Moon. Here, temperatures can be as low as -247 °C!
9. Most comets come from the Oort Cloud, which lies at the very edge of our solar system.
10. Asteroids are pieces of rock that orbit the Sun, but that are too small to be considered planets. They are only found in the inner solar system, and most of them are found the Asteroid Belt between Mars and Jupiter
11. The light from the Sun travels at 299,792 kilometres per second, and despite the 146 million kilometres that separate the Sun from the Earth, it only takes eight minutes for its light to reach us.
12. Potential candidates for places, other than Earth, where there may be life in our solar system include Mars, some of the moons of Jupiter and Saturn, and Pluto.
13. The planet with the shortest day is Jupiter. A day there lasts just under ten hours.
14. Pluto is no longer considered to be a planet because it has not managed to clear its orbit of other objects.
15. At 4,879 kilometres In diameter, the smallest planet in our solar system is Mercury.
16. The planet with the longest year is Neptune. A year there lasts 164.8 Earth years.

Where To Find Out More About Our Solar System

If you would like to learn more about our solar system, you can check out the following resources:

- **Wikipedia:** *en.wikipedia.org/wiki/Solar_System.*
- **Encyclopaedia Britannica:** *www.britannica.com/science/solar-system.*
- **The BBC:** *www.bbc.co.uk/science/space/solar system.*
- **The Wonders of the Solar System (TV Series):** Presented by Professor Brian Cox, this BBC television series is an excellent way to find out more about our solar system. It is available on DVD.
- **The Wonders of the Solar System (book):** This is an excellent book about the solar system written by Brian Cox and Andrew Cohen.

Dedication

This book is dedicated to all who love space, learning and drawing, regardless of their age!

Books available now in the *Draw Your Own Encyclopaedia* series from Pictish Beast Publications:

1. **Mammals** - ISBN: 978-1-909832-39-8. RRP: UK: £6.99 US: $8.99.
2. **Birds** - ISBN: 978-1-909832-41-1. RRP: UK: £6.99 US: $8.99.
3. **Reptiles** - ISBN: 978-1-909832-42-8. RRP: UK: £6.99 US: $8.99.
4. **Amphibians** - ISBN: 978-1-909832-43-5. RRP: UK: £6.99 US: $8.99.
5. **Fish** - ISBN: 978-1-909832-44-2. RRP: UK: £6.99 US: $8.99.
6. **Invertebrates** - ISBN: 978-1-909832-45-9. RRP: UK: £6.99 US: $8.99.
7. **Animals Box Set** – ISBN: 978-1-909832-51-0. RRP: UK: £39.99 US:$49.99.
8. **Scotland's Dolphins** - ISBN: 978-1-909832-55-8. RRP: UK: £6.99 US: $8.99.
9. **Scotland's Seabirds** - ISBN: 978-1-909832-59-6. RRP: UK: £6.99 US: $8.99.
10. **Scotland's Native Wildlife** - ISBN: 978-1-909832-59-6. RRP: UK: £6.99 US: $8.99.
11. **Scotland's Castles** - ISBN: 978-1-909832-62-6. RRP: UK: £6.99 US: $8.99.
12. **Scotland's Folklore** - ISBN: 978-1-909832-63-3. RRP: UK: £6.99 US: $8.99.
13. **Our Solar System** - ISBN: 978-1-909832-47-3. RRP: UK: £6.99 US: $8.99.

Books coming soon in the *Draw Your Own Encyclopaedia* series:

1. **Planet Earth** - ISBN: 978-1-909832-46-6. RRP: UK: £6.99 US: $8.99.
2. **Deep Space** - ISBN: 978-1-909832-48-0. RRP: UK: £6.99 US: $8.99.
3. **The Universe** - ISBN: 978-1-909832-49-7. RRP: UK: £6.99 US: $8.99.
4. **Space Exploration** - ISBN: 978-1-909832-50-3. RRP: UK: £6.99 US: $8.99.

For more information on this series of books (including a full list of available and upcoming titles), visit: *www.pictishbeastpublications.com/draw-your-own-encyclopaedia*

21207214R00020

Made in the USA
Columbia, SC
15 July 2018

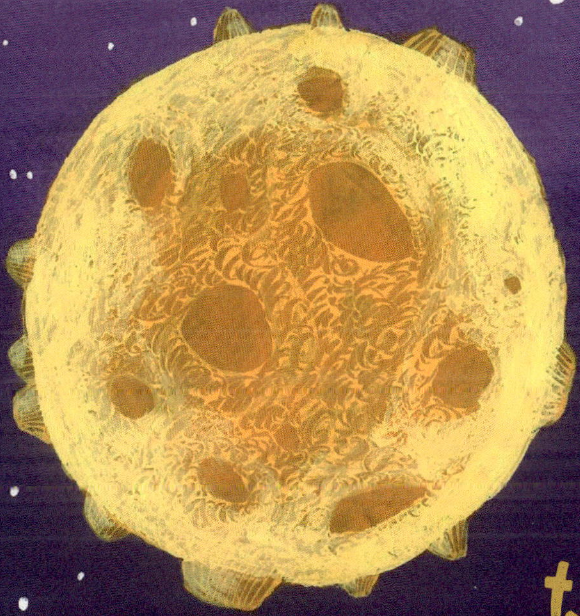

This book belongs to...

Maybe Moon Frogs

By Hayley Weeks

An IMP Book ISBN 9780955917790

www.hayleyweeks.com

A CIP catalogue record for this book is available from the British Library.

Cover title font by Krystine Bosland.

Published in the UK by
Impact Media Publishing Ltd
Registered address: 233 Wigan Rd,
Ashton-in-Makerfield,
Wigan WN4 9SR
www.impactmediapublishing.co.uk

Author's early work

Could there be frogs upon the moon?
What if we could see them soon?
What would they eat? How can they be found?
Flying, crawling or hopping around?
Open your mind and guess with your eyes,
Come with us for a big surprise.

Maybe Moon Frogs are super hairy?
Long moustaches, bearded, scary.
Grooming themselves they look quite smart,
Munching moon rocks is good for their heart.

Maybe Moon Frogs are quite a sight?
Looking splendid in black and white.
Candy canes they love to eat,
Stripy, yummy and oh so sweet!

Maybe Moon Frogs are made of steel?
Crashing and clanking seeking a meal.
Using lasers to spot their favourite treat,
Light bulbs is what they really eat!

Maybe Moon Frogs have lots of eyes?
Eating stardust from the skies.
Licking their lips with a long slimy slurp,
You'll have to forgive them if they burp!

Maybe Moon Frogs are made of cheese?
Catching food upon the breeze.
Stretching their tongues for a tasty treat,
Gobbling up the bugs that they meet.

Maybe Moon Frogs can really fly?
Gliding across the moonlit sky.
Soaring, weaving, enjoying the flight,
Chomping on stars is their delight.

Maybe Moon Frogs are carrot-like with green hair,
Creeping from their crater lair.
Grabbing what they like the most,
Scoffing lots of buttered toast.

Maybe Moon Frogs have got coloured stripes?
Greens and blues and all different types.
To fill up their rainbow tummies the best,
Chips and fried eggs, then home for a rest.

Maybe Moon Frogs are hard to see?
With their frog invisibility.
Keeping hidden away from sight,
Would you see them in the night?

When next you stare upon the moon,
Can you see them? You just might... soon!

Lightning Source UK Ltd.
Milton Keynes UK
UKIC02n2256301115
263863UK00002B/12